Free copies of the documents below that can be used with the Knowledge & Experience Grid are available from:

www.keyfax.net

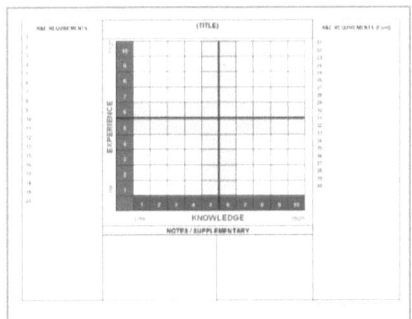

Master K&E Grid

Collation Tables

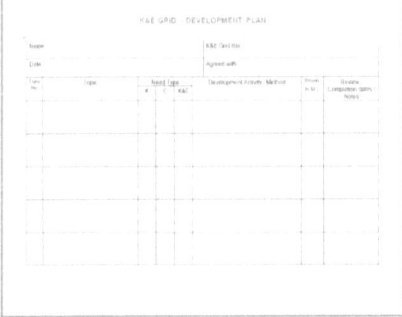

K&E Development Plan

The Knowledge & Experience Grid

The Knowledge & Experience Grid
(The K&E Grid)

John Rodwell

© John Rodwell 2014

All rights reserved. No part of this book may be used or reproduced in any manner whatsoever without written permission.

Published 2014 by Lulu.com

ISBN: 978-1-291-75741-5

Contents

Introduction to the K&E Grid 1

Why Knowledge & Experience? 2

How it works 6

    The Topics 6

    The Quadrants 6

    Scoring 7

    The Grey Boxes 10

Identifying Appropriate Development Methods 12

Producing a K&E Grid 14

    Left / Right columns 14

    Lower Boxes 15

An Example Grid 17

Analysing an individual's K&E grid 21

Producing a Development Plan 25

Collating Multiple K&E Grids 27

Analysing the Results 30

Evaluation & Follow-up 32

Introduction to the K&E Grid

A K&E Grid is a tool for managers, trainers, HR professionals and consultants for the identification of learning and development needs for managers and employees at any level.

Its main features and advantages are that it:
- is simple to use
- can accurately identify training and other development needs
- provides a very visual indication of what the key areas for development are
- can indicate how the identified need can be effectively met
- promotes focused discussions between managers and their staff
- can all be done on one side of A4 paper
- can also enable team or group development needs to be shown on one side of A4 paper
- prevents wasting time and money on staff development that isn't really needed

The tool invites individuals to consider each item from a numbered list of job-related topics and then assess themselves on their levels of knowledge and experience for each of them. This is then plotted onto the grid by writing or typing-in the relevant topic numbers.

When each item on the list has been plotted onto the grid it will reveal the main areas where development is needed. It will also reveal where no development is needed because the individual's knowledge and experience levels relating to the topics are sufficiently high already.

The illustration on the next page shows how a grid can look before being filled in by the respondents.

The Knowledge & Experience Grid

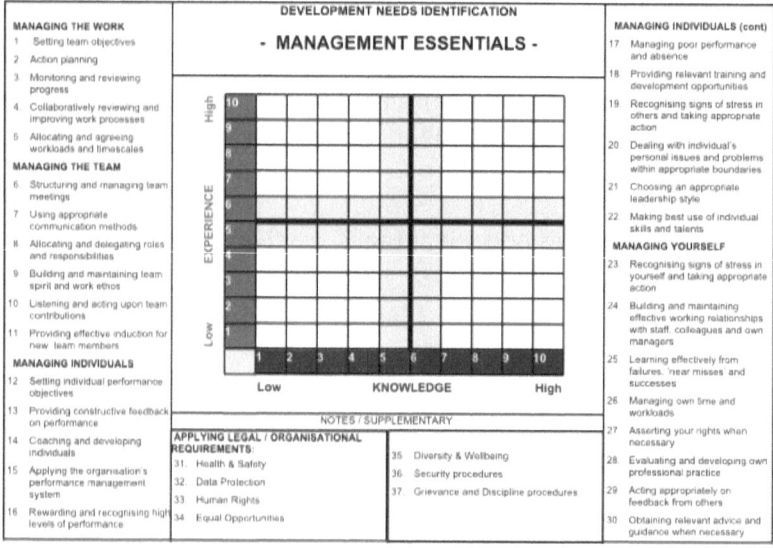

Why Knowledge & Experience?

In the field of Learning and Development, the term 'Knowledge & Skills' is one that is used much more frequently than Knowledge & Experience. A development, learning or training needs analysis will often be phrased in a way that aims to identify the 'gap' between the actual and required levels of people's knowledge and skill. This terminology however does not work as effectively as Knowledge & Experience with regard to the grid as explained below.

If for example you ask someone if they have the knowledge and skills to 'Set and agree team objectives', they may answer yes. This answer could be reasonably based on the fact that they know the theory of how to write effective team objectives, and believe that they have the communication skills necessary to agree them with team members.

The Knowledge & Experience Grid

Ask them however if they actually have any *experience* of setting and agreeing team objectives, and they may well answer in the negative. This could therefore constitute a development need in order to put the existing knowledge and skills into practice to gain the *experience*, which in turn leads to greater *understanding* which is much more likely to bring benefits to the individuals, and the organisation.

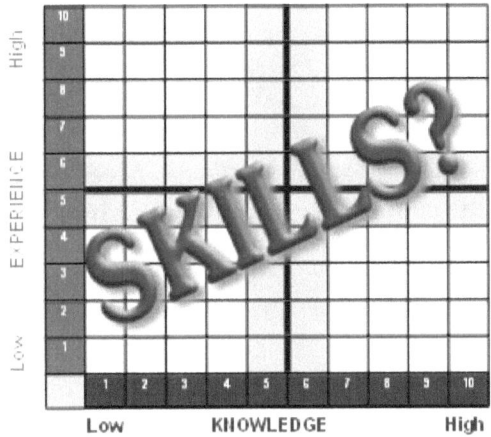

'Experience' therefore equates to 'Skills' to an extent, but goes further in the sense that it relates to the actual application of the knowledge and skills in a real, live, work environment.

If a needs analysis is based on experience, the assessment is likely to be more objective. It can be assessed by virtue of identifying the approximate or actual number of times the knowledge and skill has been applied. It is more of a quantitative, rather than a qualitative assessment of the application of knowledge and skill.

In the workplace, it is the *application* of learned knowledge and skills that is needed to bring about the necessary benefits after any developmental activity. Having particular knowledge and skills is of no use if they are not applied. The longer the break between the learning and its application, the less will be remembered. 'Use it or lose it' as the saying goes. If an individual has not had the opportunity to put what they have learned into practice and gain the relevant experience, there may still be a development need.

Another reason for using 'Experience' is that gaining experience is a form of development that can sometimes be overlooked. It is a term that also opens up a potentially wider range of development opportunities for the learner.

If the learning of certain *skills* is necessary for an individual, the common initial option is a training course or e-learning package that teaches the skills. This may be a valid option for learning particular technical skills (such as IT etc.) However, if the skills are more personal or interpersonal, it will be more effective to couch the need in terms of *experience*.

If this is done, options such as coaching / project work / working closely with an experienced colleague / taking on new or additional responsibilities / doing someone else's job for a while all become potentially valid ways of learning that do not involve a training course.

According to Princeton University around 70% of peoples' real learning of how to do their jobs effectively comes from the experience of doing it. 20% comes informal learning from others and reading / discussions and so on and just 10% from formal learning activities (courses / e-learning and so on). This has become known as the '70/20/10 Rule'.

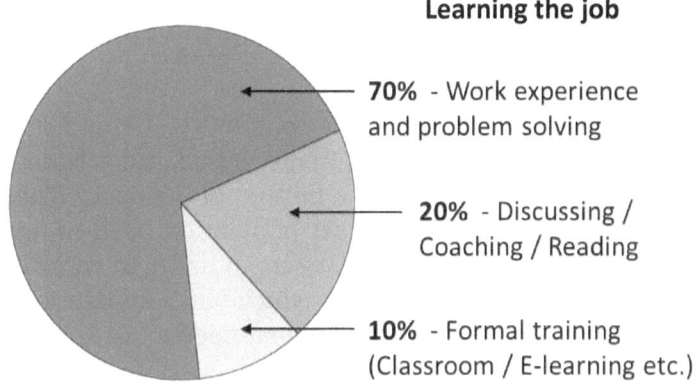

Learning the job

70% - Work experience and problem solving

20% - Discussing / Coaching / Reading

10% - Formal training (Classroom / E-learning etc.)

Therefore, identifying development needs through measuring the level of experience that people have, and meeting the needs through the gaining of experience through workplace learning activities is likely to have a much more significant impact on individual and organisational performance.

Using the K&E Grid will also enable you to identify people who have high levels of knowledge and experience in certain areas. You can then use such people as coaches or instructors to help enhance the quality of the 20% of learning achieved through workplace discussions and coaching. You can find a suitable matches therefore of people who need to learn how to do things, with people who can show them.

How it works

The Topics

The two columns on each side contain numbered lists of topics (with some additional items circled in the 'Notes' / Supplementary section at the bottom of the page). These are the topics that your target population need to have both knowledge and experience in, in order to carry out their roles effectively, and for which you are identifying particular learning and development needs.

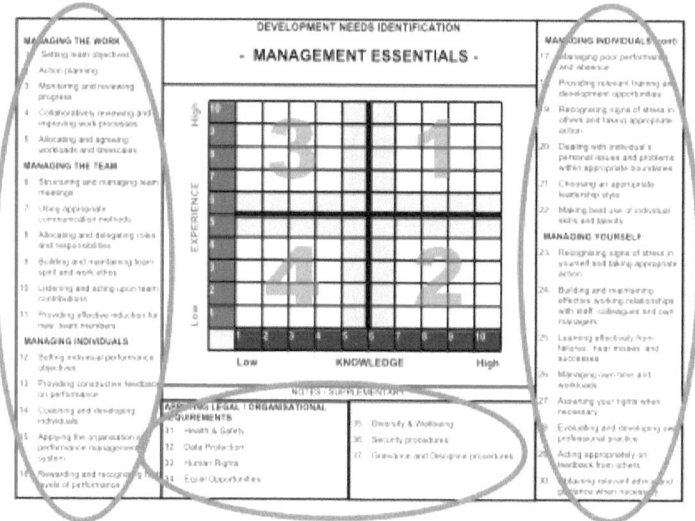

The Quadrants

As shown by the Knowledge and Experience axes and the bold lines, the grid can be divided into four quadrants

Quadrant 1: High Knowledge / High Experience
Quadrant 2: High Knowledge / Low Experience
Quadrant 3: Low Knowledge / High Experience
Quadrant 4: Low Knowledge / Low Experience

The Knowledge & Experience Grid

Scoring

If, for example, you are completing the grid, you need to consider each of the numbered topics and decide how much knowledge, and how much experience you have in relation to it.

For each item you can score yourself from 1 – 10 on the Knowledge scale and then the same on the Experience scale.

If you consider that for **topic No. 1** you have quite a lot of knowledge about it, but have rarely put that knowledge into practice to become experienced, you might score yourself with 7 on the Knowledge scale, and 2 on the Experience scale (K7 - E2). You will therefore type or write '**1**' on the grid in the position shown below.

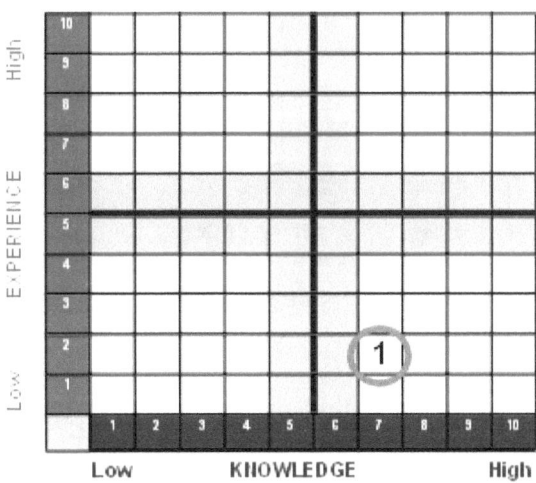

As another example, for **topic No. 2** on the list, you might have been carrying out the activity for some time, but would like to increase or update your knowledge on it.

You might think that there is some knowledge that you are missing, or that there may have been changes and developments that you are not aware of, or you are not sure that you have been doing the job as efficiently as you could have.

In such cases you might score yourself with an 8 on the Experience scale, and a 4 on the Knowledge scale (K4 - E8). Your score for topic No.2 would therefore be placed as shown below.

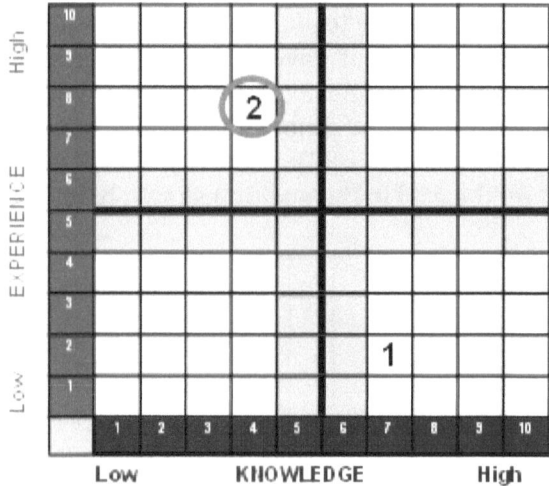

A problem with identifying a need for knowledge is that often 'You don't know what you don't know'.

Therefore, you do not necessarily need to be aware of exactly what it is you don't know. You might initially just want to find out *if* there is any extra knowledge that might be available to you.

If you think there will be some additional knowledge that will be of benefit to doing your job, then place your score on the lower scale.

The Knowledge & Experience Grid

For topic No. 3 you may have a lot of knowledge and experience in this area, so you would therefore place the topic number in a position something like where the No. 3 is (K8 - E9).

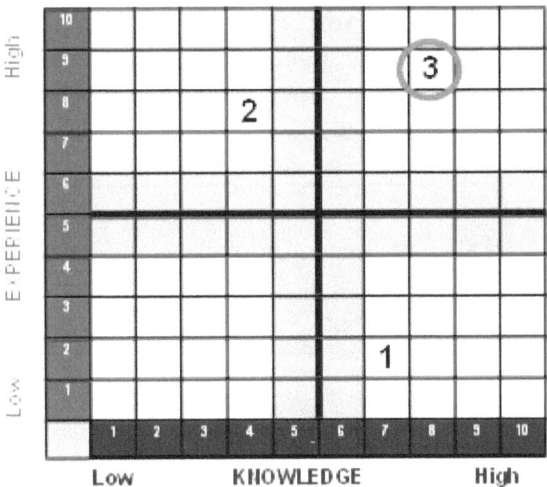

If on the other hand, you have little knowledge and little experience, the topic number would be placed somewhere like where No. 4 is (K2 - E3).

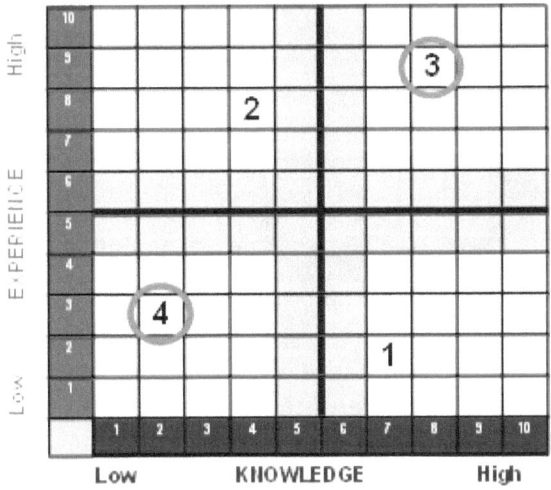

The Knowledge & Experience Grid

Topics in quadrant 4 will often indicate a priority development need, although this may not always be the case if the topic is not an essential feature of the job.

On the actual document, you would continue this process for all of the topics until you have them all plotted somewhere on the grid. (Unless the topic is not relevant to your area of work, in which case you need not place its number on the grid at all).

> The plotting of the topic numbers does not have to be made with absolute accuracy in all cases. The key point is that you place each number in an appropriate *quadrant* (or in a grey box - see below)

The Grey Boxes

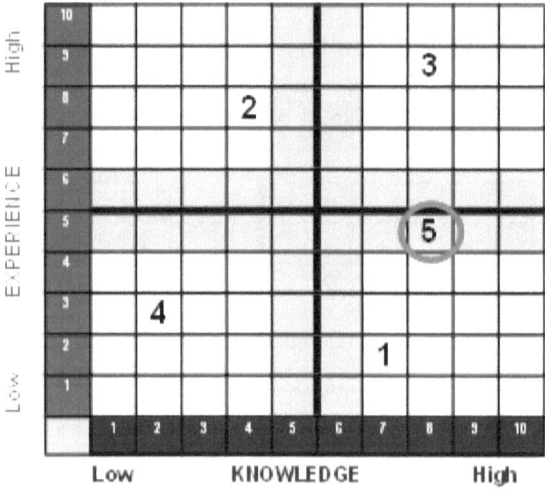

The grey boxes on the grid are where you can place any topic numbers you are uncertain about and which may require further consideration or discussion. These represent the 'borderline' topics where you are not sure

The Knowledge & Experience Grid

about your knowledge or experience levels, or you may not even be sure about what the *meaning* of the numbered topic, and you need to seek clarification.

You can discuss these 'grey' topics with others, or you manager to help place them into a more definite quadrant when you can.

As an example, a topic number inserted into a grey box at K8-E5 would indicate that you have quite a high knowledge level, but you have some doubt that your experience level is high enough and you want to discuss or consider it further.

Identifying Appropriate Development Methods

The K&E Grid enables the identification of the possible best method to meet the identified gaps in either experience or knowledge. The appropriate form of development will be indicated by whatever quadrant the topic has been placed in:

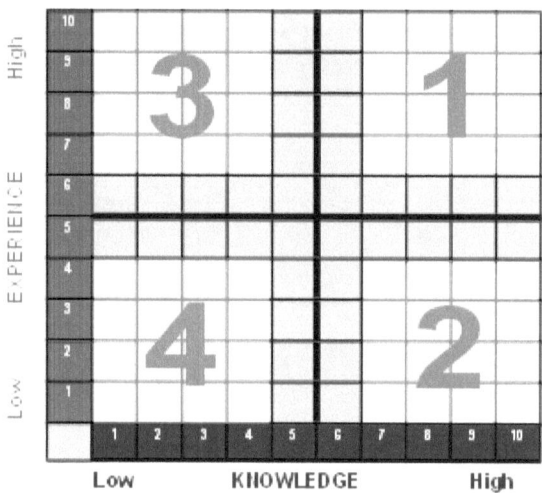

Quadrant 1 - High Knowledge / High Experience
If you have placed a topic number here, the indication is that there are no further development needs necessary. However, this does discount the possibility that you may want to develop your knowledge or experience even further into becoming a recognised specialist in the field.

Quadrant 2 - High Knowledge / Low Experience
If you place a topic number in this quadrant, the indication is that you have sufficient knowledge about the topic, but you have not had the opportunity to use that knowledge in a 'live' situation in order to gain a reasonable level of experience.

It is likely therefore that the need for further experience can best be met by participating in a relevant project or activity (possibly with an experienced colleague) being coached by a colleague or manager, or obtaining some specific skills-based training, where you can put the knowledge you have into practice.

Quadrant 3 - Low Knowledge / High Experience
An item placed in Quadrant 3 would indicate that some private study or reading, researching on the Internet, or obtaining information from a knowledgeable person would be some of the possible options to 'top up' the knowledge you need. As mentioned earlier, this represents the situation where you may have been doing the work for years, but remain uncertain as to whether you have been doing it the 'proper' way, or where you are sure that there is still more to be known about the topic.

Quadrant 4 - Low Knowledge / Low Experience
If you have an item placed in Quadrant 4, this would indicate the need for some kind of development programme that would provide both knowledge and skills practice. This could subsequently be followed by an assignment, project or coaching to put the learning into practice and gain sufficient experience.

Producing a K&E Grid

A K&E Grid begins with the template shown below

The template is made up of the actual grid in the centre which is a table of 11 columns and 11 rows, lined, numbered, coloured and shaded as you can see above with the High / Low Knowledge and Experience scales typed into text boxes and positioned accordingly.

At the top of the grid is a text box for the title and the nature of the learning and development needs being identified. It can also be used to show the name of the person completing the grid and the date and so on.

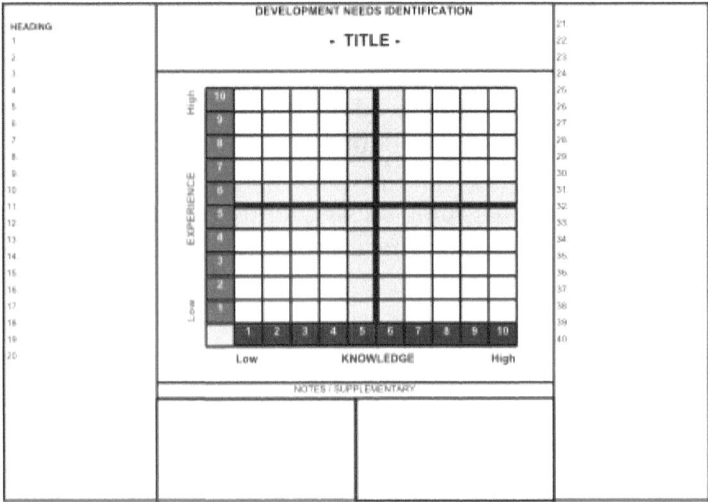

Left / Right columns

To the left and right of the grid are columns made from text boxes with numbers down each side. The template has numbers 1 - 20 in the left hand column, and 21 - 40 in the right hand column. These numbers will vary depending on the number of topics you need to include in the final grid.

The next task is to populate the two main numbered columns with topics. This will of course depend upon the nature of the needs analysis you wish to undertake.

Such lists can come from a range of sources such as:

- Competence frameworks
- Job descriptions
- Job / task analyses or desk notes
- Existing training prospectuses
- National Occupational Standards
- Local / organisational standards or operating procedures
- Internet or other research
- Brainstorming / own knowledge

The wording of these lists is a vital consideration. Each item *must* be an action that can be carried out. (It must be something that an individual can gain experience in). The items should also be written as briefly and succinctly as possible.

You can test if a topic has been suitably worded if it enables the following two questions to be answered:

1. *"To what extent do you know how to do this effectively?"*

2. *"How much experience do you have of actually doing this?"*

Lower Boxes

At the bottom of the grid are text boxes for any notes or additional / supplementary topics you may want to include.

These text boxes could also be used for topics that involve the learning of knowledge only. These could include knowledge of models and theories that support the effective completion of the job. For example:

1. Theories of motivation (Maslow, Herzberg, McClelland etc.)
2. Theories of Group Development
3. Theories of Adult Learning

If such knowledge topics are used, they should be numbered separately (such as K1, K2, K3 and so on) and scored only along the *bottom* line of the grid.

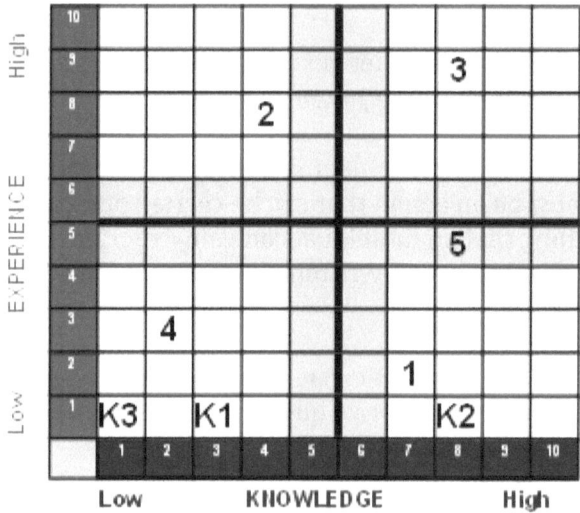

If you are producing different K&E Grids for different job roles, but there are some common topics, give the common topics the same number across all the relevant grids. This will make the collation and identification of the learning needs very much easier. You can use the lower boxes of the K&E Grid for common topics and/or number them as C1, C2 and so on.

An Example Grid

A large example K&E Grid is shown on the following page. This shows a list of topics under the title of 'Management Essentials'. This list is based on the CIPD/ACAS 'Five a Day' competences that most managers need to be able to demonstrate. In this example the lower boxes have been used to show particular legal and organisational policy topics.

When the grid has been populated with the needs analysis topics, it can be copied and distributed to the relevant individuals and groups with the instructions and any necessary background information you may need to provide.

The K&E Grids should be issued to individual employees for completion. From the results, individual development needs can be discussed, identified, prioritised and planned with each individual's line manager.

Group needs can also be identified and prioritised if copies of the individually completed grids are copied and collected. A later section will cover the collation of batches of K&E grids.

The Knowledge & Experience Grid

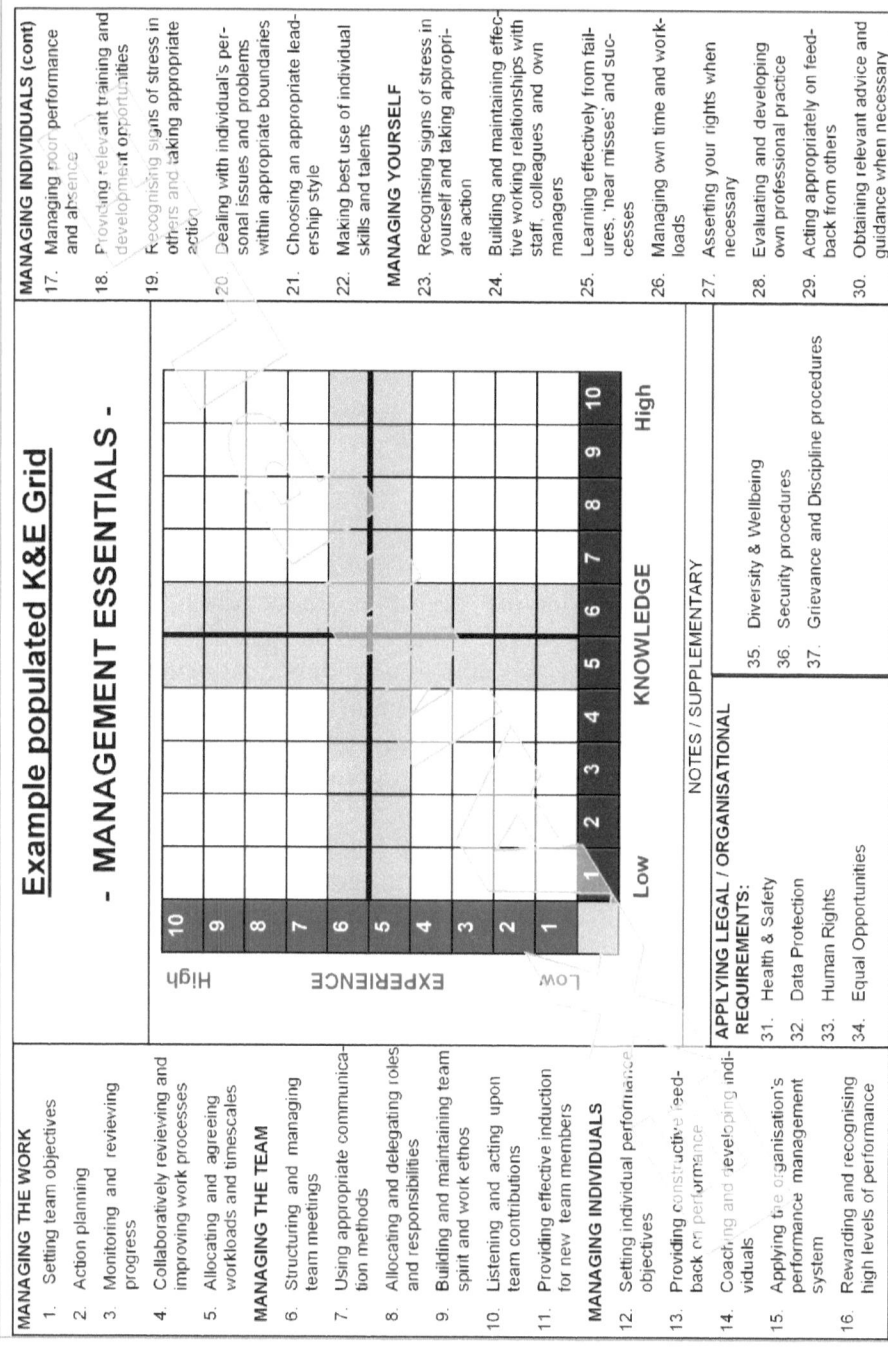

Example populated K&E Grid
- MANAGEMENT ESSENTIALS -

MANAGING THE WORK
1. Setting team objectives
2. Action planning
3. Monitoring and reviewing progress
4. Collaboratively reviewing and improving work processes
5. Allocating and agreeing workloads and timescales

MANAGING THE TEAM
6. Structuring and managing team meetings
7. Using appropriate communication methods
8. Allocating and delegating roles and responsibilities
9. Building and maintaining team spirit and work ethos
10. Listening and acting upon team contributions
11. Providing effective induction for new team members

MANAGING INDIVIDUALS
12. Setting individual performance objectives
13. Providing constructive feedback on performance
14. Coaching and developing individuals
15. Applying the organisation's performance management system
16. Rewarding and recognising high levels of performance

MANAGING INDIVIDUALS (cont)
17. Managing poor performance and absence
18. Providing relevant training and development opportunities
19. Recognising signs of stress in others and taking appropriate action
20. Dealing with individual's personal issues and problems within appropriate boundaries
21. Choosing an appropriate leadership style
22. Making best use of individual skills and talents

MANAGING YOURSELF
23. Recognising signs of stress in yourself and taking appropriate action
24. Building and maintaining effective working relationships with staff, colleagues and own managers
25. Learning effectively from failures, 'near misses' and successes
26. Managing own time and workloads
27. Asserting your rights when necessary
28. Evaluating and developing own professional practice
29. Acting appropriately on feedback from others
30. Obtaining relevant advice and guidance when necessary

APPLYING LEGAL / ORGANISATIONAL REQUIREMENTS:
31. Health & Safety
32. Data Protection
33. Human Rights
34. Equal Opportunities

NOTES / SUPPLEMENTARY
35. Diversity & Wellbeing
36. Security procedures
37. Grievance and Discipline procedures

The Knowledge & Experience Grid

The illustration below shows the example grid completed by a manager within an organisation.

Example populated K&E Grid
- MANAGEMENT ESSENTIALS -

	Low									High
High 10										
9										
8					26					
EXPERIENCE 7			3		22					
6										
5				4			16	17		27
4			32 33							13
3			14				19	7 37		34
2								23		2 11
Low 1	1	2	3	4	5	6	7	8	9	10

(faint entries in upper rows: 10, 13, 6 20; 24; 29 30, 25, 15; 5, 8 31 35; 9)

KNOWLEDGE

NOTES / SUPPLEMENTARY

APPLYING LEGAL / ORGANISATIONAL REQUIREMENTS:
31. Health & Safety
32. Data Protection
33. Human Rights
34. Equal Opportunities
35. Diversity & Wellbeing
36. Security procedures
37. Grievance and Discipline procedures

MANAGING THE WORK
1. Setting team objectives
2. Action planning
3. Monitoring and reviewing progress
4. Collaboratively reviewing and improving work processes
5. Allocating and agreeing workloads and timescales

MANAGING THE TEAM
6. Structuring and managing team meetings
7. Using appropriate communication methods
8. Allocating and delegating roles and responsibilities
9. Building and maintaining team spirit and work ethos
10. Listening and acting upon team contributions
11. Providing effective induction for new team members

MANAGING INDIVIDUALS
12. Setting individual performance objectives
13. Providing constructive feedback on performance
14. Coaching and developing individuals
15. Applying the organisation's performance management system
16. Rewarding and recognising high levels of performance

MANAGING INDIVIDUALS (cont)
17. Managing poor performance and absence
18. Providing relevant training and development opportunities
19. Recognising signs of stress in others and taking appropriate action
20. Dealing with individual's personal issues and problems within appropriate boundaries
21. Choosing an appropriate leadership style
22. Making best use of individual skills and talents

MANAGING YOURSELF
23. Recognising signs of stress in yourself and taking appropriate action
24. Building and maintaining effective working relationships with staff, colleagues and own managers
25. Learning effectively from failures, near misses and successes
26. Managing own time and workloads
27. Asserting your rights when necessary
28. Evaluating and developing own professional practice
29. Acting appropriately on feedback from others
30. Obtaining relevant advice and guidance when necessary

As you can see, there are entries in all four quadrants. Some boxes contain two numbers where the same scores apply.

If there are third or fourth topic numbers to be inserted which will not fit without distorting the box size, they can be placed in an adjacent box. As mentioned earlier, the key issue is to get each topic number in the correct quadrant.

You can set up the grid to be colour-coded to reflect the nature of the needs. For example:

Quadrant 1 (HK / HE)
Green - like a 'go' traffic light

Quadrant 2 (HK / LE)
The same colour as the Experience box shading - to indicate that the need is for Experience

Quadrant 3 (LK / HE)
The same colour as the Knowledge box shading - to indicate a need for Knowledge

Quadrant 4 (LK / LE)
Red - to indicate a warning that there could be a priority need.

This kind of colour coding can be set up easily if you are producing the grid as a table on Microsoft Word. Just select the boxes and choose the text colour you want.

You could use further colour coding if you wish for the grey boxes.

The Knowledge & Experience Grid

Analysing an individual's K&E Grid

Looking at the completed grid again, you can start to identify what the needs are, and use the information as part of a development discussion.

In this example we can identify some discussion points working backwards from the areas of apparent greatest need:

Quadrant 4 (LK / LE) - Needs knowledge and experience in collaboratively reviewing and improving work processes, and coaching and developing individuals (topics 4 and 14).

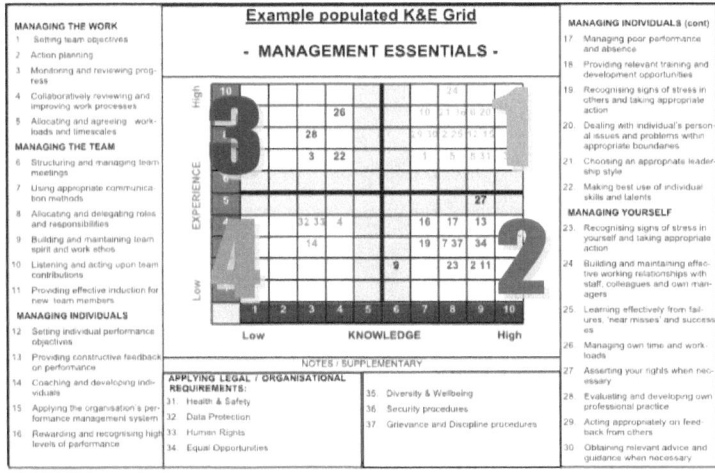

To meet these needs, some formal training might be appropriate (e.g. On coaching and developing individuals) whilst the collaborative reviewing and improving work processes might best be developed through coaching by the manager's manager.

Topics 32 and 33 however (Data Protection and Human Rights) are less easy to pin down in terms of the 'experience' that may be needed. A possible approach could therefore be to gain some basic knowledge about these topics first, and then see how, when or even *if*, the knowledge can be effectively applied in the workplace.

Quadrant 3 (LK / HE) - These four topics indicate that the manager may have being doing these things for a while, but remains uncertain as to whether they have been done as well as they could have been. They may feel that there is something 'missing' from their knowledge and that there is possibly a better or different way.

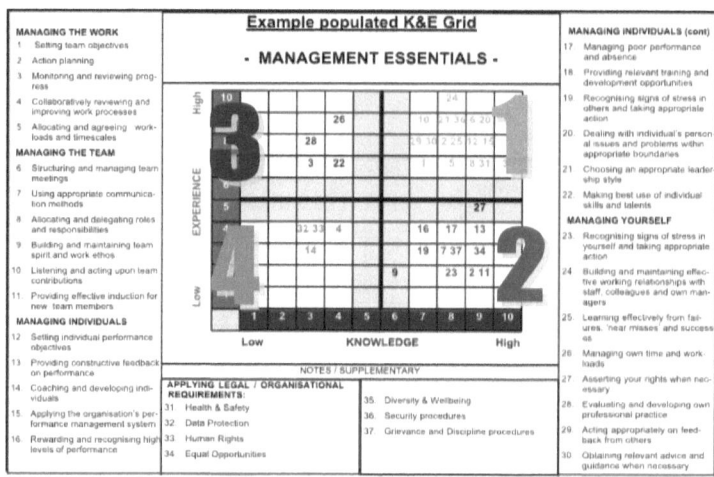

With topics like these, there may be some formal processes available that could be identified through things like self-study, internet research, or checking with the HR department.

Quadrant 2 (HK / LE) - There are quite a few topic numbers in this quadrant. Some may indicate an immediate priority need, others not. For example, the manager has high knowledge of providing induction for new team members (topic 11), but just simply may not have any new team members appointed. Therefore, no setting-up of a development opportunity for the manager would really be necessary. Other topics in this category could be those for managing poor performance and absence (topic 17) and grievance and discipline procedures (topic 37).

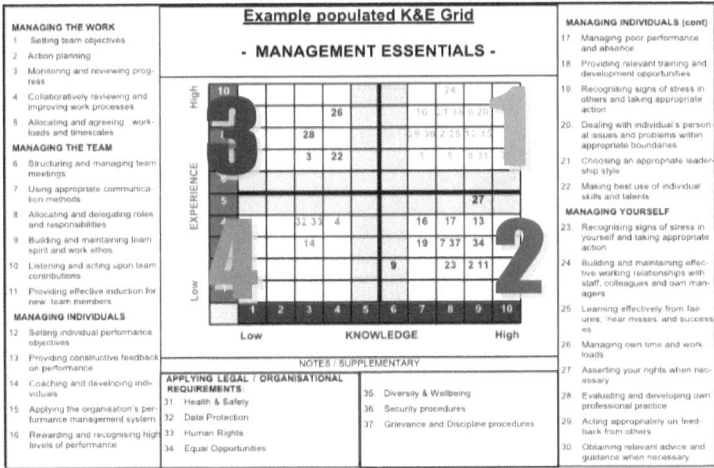

In these circumstances, no immediate action would be needed. However, should a new team member arrive, or a poor performance situation arises, the manager's actions could be monitored to ensure that their knowledge was put into practice effectively and correctly.

On the other hand, using appropriate communication skills (topic 7) and providing constructive feedback on performance (topic 13) could be considered as essential skills to be demonstrated on an almost daily basis, and therefore needing some opportunities to put the knowledge into practice to gain more experience in these areas.

As these are skills that are needed, which have to be put into practice at the workplace, some formal training might be appropriate for these two topics.

The Knowledge & Experience Grid

Quadrant 1 (HK / HE) - The discussion around these topics should be to confirm that they have been realistically placed in this quadrant. Some *evidence* of the manager's knowledge and experience could be sought and/or provided to help the confirmation.

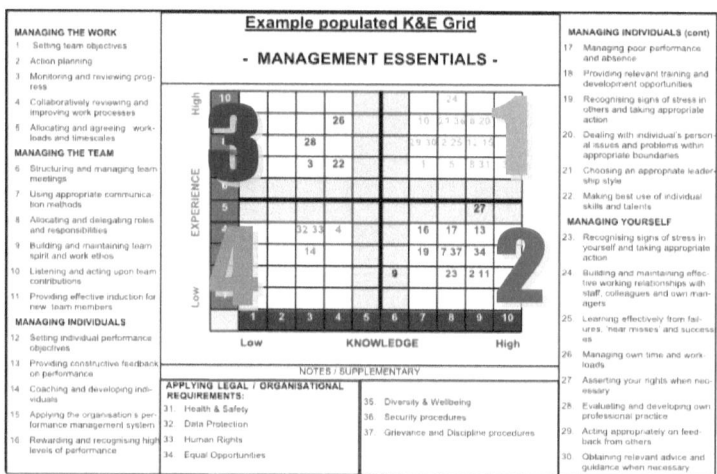

Grey Boxes - In this example, the manager has identified building and maintaining team spirit and ethos (topic 9) and asserting own rights (topic 27) as requiring more discussion. Some feedback and evidence from the manager's own team and the manager's manager or peers could help to move these topics into a more definite quadrant.

Producing a Development Plan

When an individual's K&E Grid has been completed, a development plan can be drawn up to highlight the priority development needs.

A possible format for development plan is shown below. It shows references back to the K&E Grid and the types of need specified as relating to knowledge, experience, or both. The topic numbers, topic name and types of need can be transferred directly from the K&E Grid.

Name:					K&E Grid title		
Date:					Agreed with		
Topic No.	Topic	Need Type			Development Activity / Method	Priority H M L	Review /Completion dates / Notes
		K	E	K&E			

A larger example is shown on the following page.

Usually, the most beneficial approach is for the individual who has completed the K&E Grid to then go on and produce a draft development plan to discuss with their manager.

The Knowledge & Experience Grid

Name:		K&E Grid title				
Date:		Agreed with				
Topic No.	Topic	Need Type (K / E / K&E)	Development Activity / Method	Priority H M L	Review /Completion dates / Notes	

Collating Multiple K&E Grids

A number of K&E Grids covering the same topics can be brought together and collated to identify the learning and development needs of the groups or teams that have completed them. For example, where a group of managers complete grids like the earlier example and copies of them are batched for collation.

As with the individual grids, a collation sheet can be produced to show the collated results on a single side of A4 paper.

The collation table is made up of 4 main quadrants to match those of the K&E Grid. Each quadrant is then divided into 3, 4 or 5 columns of 10 rows.

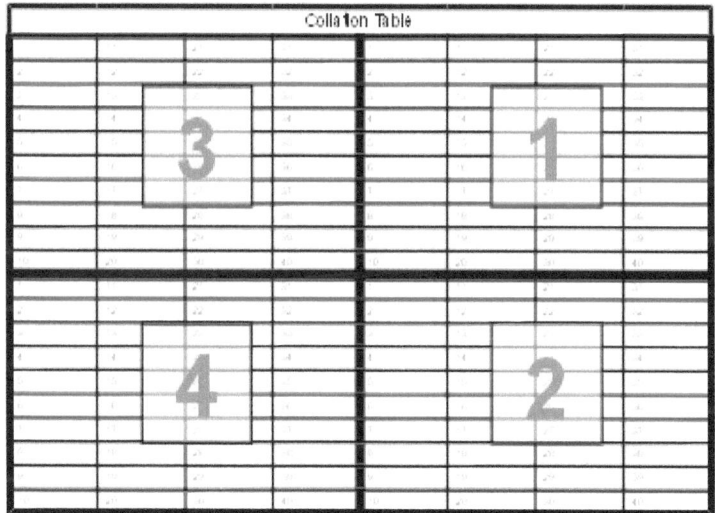

The number of columns will depend on the number of topics you have on the K&E Grid. If, for example, you have a total number of 37 topics (as in the Management Essentials example) then a total number of 40 boxes in each quadrant will be appropriate. The boxes are then

The Knowledge & Experience Grid

numbered, and these represent the topic numbers on the K&E Grid.

When collating a batch of K&E Grids, the respondents' scores are simply transferred onto the Collation Table using a 5-bar-gate type system. Therefore, if a respondent has scored Topic No. 1 as High Knowledge / High Experience then a mark is made in box number 1 in Quadrant 1 on the collation table. If they then have Topic No. 2 in Quadrant 3, then a mark is made in box number 2 in Quadrant 3. This is done for all respondents for all topics, and eventually a table will be built up to show the group results.

The example below shows a completed Collation Table for a 38-topic K&E Grid with 10 respondents. A larger blank Collation Table is shown on the next page.

The Knowledge & Experience Grid

Collation Table - Project:							
1	11	21	31	1	11	21	31
2	12	22	32	2	12	22	32
3	13	23	33	3	13	23	33
4	14	24	34	4	14	24	34
5	15	25	35	5	15	25	35
6	16	26	36	6	16	26	36
7	17	27	37	7	17	27	37
8	18	28	38	8	18	28	38
9	19	29	39	9	19	29	39
10	20	30	40	10	20	30	40
1	11	21	31	1	11	21	31
2	12	22	32	2	12	22	32
3	13	23	33	3	13	23	33
4	14	24	34	4	14	24	34
5	15	25	35	5	15	25	35
6	16	26	36	6	16	26	36
7	17	27	37	7	17	27	37
8	18	28	38	8	18	28	38
9	19	29	39	9	19	29	39
10	20	30	40	10	20	30	40

Analysing the Results

The individuals who completed the K&E Grids will probably gain the most from discussing their own grids with their managers, and planning and prioritising their development.

At an organisational or team level however, some group needs can be identified from analysing the Collation Table and seeking to identify where one training or development opportunity might meet the needs of a significant percentage of the group, rather than individuals receiving the development individually, at potentially much higher cost.

The simplest way to identify possible group needs is to look for a high number of marks in Quadrants 2, 3 and 4.

Using the example Collation Table from the previous page, reproduced above, some group needs (and ways of meeting them) could be:

Quadrant 2: Topics 3, 10, 14, 20, 21, 26 - Coaching, work activities or skills development to help provide experience. (The coaching could be provided by people with high knowledge and experience in the topics).

Quadrant 3: Topics 2, 9, 17, 22, 25, 30, 35 - Possible knowledge-based session, production or purchase of workbooks or e-learning to cover one or more of these topics. Workshop or Action Learning set to identify and confirm best practice.

Quadrant 4: Topics 5, 23, 33 - A development programme to cover knowledge and skills requirements or 'blended' combination of learning opportunities (e.g. e-learning + course + follow-up coaching etc)

Those with Knowledge needs for the same topics in quadrants 3 and 4 could attend or receive the same learning and development activities.

> When the Collation Table has been completed, it will also provide you with a snapshot of the current levels of knowledge and experience that you have across the organisation (or relevant part of it). It will therefore give you a form of 'Skills Audit' that could be useful for other resource planning purposes

Evaluation & Follow-up

A K&E Grid can also be used as a follow-up evaluation tool to identify the extent to which any learning and development has increased the individual's or group's levels of knowledge and experience.

If a second, identical, grid is distributed and completed by the same people between 3 - 6 months after the first, you should see a movement towards people indicating higher levels of knowledge and experience than when the grid was first completed.

Once again, the K&E Grid, and the Collation Table will provide you with an immediate *visual* indication of the increase in respondents knowledge and experience, as the examples illustrate.

You should hope to see a significant movement towards Quadrant 1 from all the other quadrants, with also a move from Quadrant 4 to Quadrant 2, which will indicate that at least the respondent's knowledge levels have increased even though they may not yet have had the opportunities to gain the experience.

Other publications by the author:

ISBN:0-566-07444-3

ISBN:0-566-087776-7

Visit: www.keyfax.net

www.ingramcontent.com/pod-product-compliance
Lightning Source LLC
Chambersburg PA
CBHW021940170526
45157CB00005B/2374